HARVEST HOUSE
PUBLISHERS
EUGENE, OREGON 97402

Simpler Times Blank Book

Copyright 1997 Thomas Kinkade, Media Arts Group, Inc, San Jose, CA
Published by Harvest House Publishers
Eugene, Oregon 97402

ISBN 0-7369-0580-4

    Media Arts Group, Inc.
    521 Charcot Avenue
    San Jose, CA 95131
    1-800-366-3733

Text is adapted from *Simpler Times* by Thomas Kinkade
(Harvest House Publishers, 1996).

Printed in China

Design and production by
Koechel Peterson & Associates, Minneapolis, Minnesota.

00 01 02 03 04 /IM / 10 9 8 7 6 5 4 3 2

From the time I was very small, I carried a sketchbook with me when I went on a hike or a long bike ride. I loved to loll on the golden hillsides and sketch lumpy green oak trees or the patterns of the clouds. I memorized sights and sounds. I collected experiences. I lived in the moment, with tomorrow always tantalizing around the bend.

As I grew older, I took my paints outdoors as well. I began the practice of plein-air painting—which simply means painting on location, out of doors. Plein-air painting forces me to experience nature on its own terms. When I am painting a scene, I'm not just walking through it or skating through it or skiing down it. I am sitting still for hours at a time, soaking it in, observing the details, breathing the air, and listening to the sounds. I am becoming a part of the natural world and letting it become a part of me.

But you don't have to be a painter to have this same experience. You can be a bird watcher. You can take a journal to a little park behind your house. You can take a walk in the woods or a drive out to a desert spring.

The point is to be quiet and receptive, to watch and listen for nature's message. Listen to the trees, for what they have to say to you. Listen to the ocean, to the many-voiced stories the waves tell. And listen to the sun, the moon, the stars, to the echoing, intimate voice of the heavens.

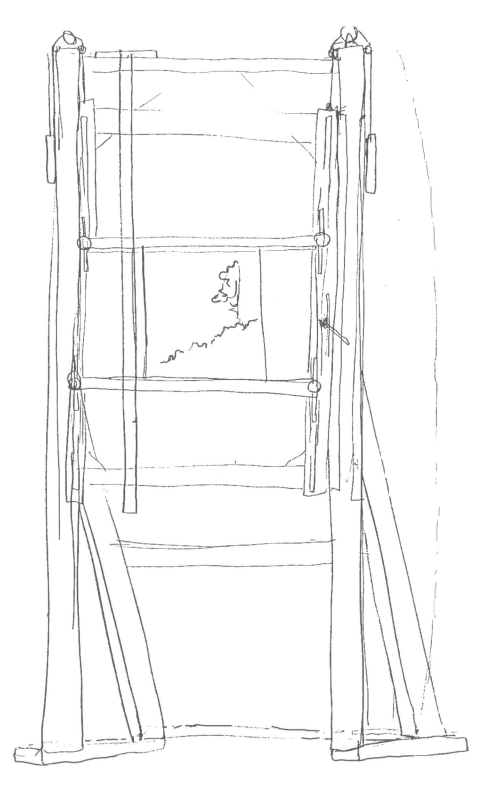

2/7/23

Dear mom,

I am sorry, I Did not mean to make you mad. It was a Joke. I Didn't talk to you because I Did not know why you were mad and was scared you would be more if I talked. I am scared to tell you it was a Joke because I Do not think you will believe me.

~

It is the simple things of life that make living worthwhile,
the sweet fundamental things such as love and duty,
work and rest and living close to nature.

LAURA INGALLS WILDER

~

Life is measured by the number
of things you are alive to.

MALTBIE D. BABCOCK

~

Let the form of an object
be what it may—light, shade, and perspective
will always make it beautiful.

JOHN CONSTABLE

~

An artist is by definition a collector of experience. And there's always another vista around the bend, beckoning an artist to see a new and different part of the world. It was while I was a student that I started the practice of going on "hoists" with my friend James Gurney. "Hoists" was our makeshift word for a sketching adventure—an excursion with sketchpads to a mountaintop, a train yard, a small town. We relished the surprise and adventure of it. We never knew where we would end up. And we filled our sketchbooks and our memories with unforgettable people and places.

~

~

I went to the woods because I wished to live deliberately, to front only the essential facts of life, and see if I could not learn what it had to teach, and not, when I came to die, discover that I had not lived.

HENRY DAVID THOREAU

~

~

~

It is only with the heart that one can see rightly;
what is essential is invisible to the eye.

ANTOINE DE SAINT-EXUPÉRY

And this our life…finds tongues in trees, books in the running
brooks, sermons in stones, and good in everything.

WILLIAM SHAKESPEARE

It is true in painting, and it's true in life: How things look depends on the way you see them. And both a well-received painting and a fulfilling life depend upon keeping a true perspective.

In art, perspective is both a viewpoint and a technique. Perspective is the lens and angle from which the painter views the world of the painting, and it is also a set of skills that enable the artist to paint that world believably. I can emphasize certain elements, minimize others, even add or subtract items, using my perspective skills to work these elements into a believable and, I hope, beautiful whole.

And yes, all this applies to perspective in life as well as in paintings. Our perspective or viewpoint involves the way we look at life. But our perspective also shapes our living.

If I am looking at life through a perspective of gratitude and hope, for instance, I will live and think differently than if my view was one of bitterness and anger. The same is true of the way I look at myself. If I maintain a balanced perspective on me—honestly recognizing my flaws and shortcomings, honestly appreciating my gifts and talents—I will live accordingly, and this balanced view will shape my life.

Fix your thoughts on what is true and good and right. Think about things that are pure and lovely, and dwell on the fine, good things in others.

THE BOOK OF PHILIPPIANS

~

Stones and trees speak slowly and may take a week to get out
a single sentence, and there are few men, unfortunately, with
the patience to wait for an oak to finish a thought.

GARRISON KEILLOR

~

~

~

Our creativity will become our prayer, born of simple attention
to what is around, and enhancing the world by its expression.

ELIZABETH J. CANHAM

~

~

~

~

~

Afoot and light-hearted I take to the open road,
Healthy, free, the world before me,
The long brown path before me leading wherever I choose.

WALT WHITMAN

~

~

～

The essence of the true view is that each of us is blessed beyond what we could ask or think, if we just take the time to realize it. Each of us can thank God for the indescribable gift that is life. To be living is to be handed a precious white canvas upon which each of us can create a painting of great depth and meaning. A painting that can be full of joy and peace. The beautiful painting of our lives.

Each life is a masterpiece in the making. And if your perspective is true, the whole canvas will be beautiful.

The real voyage of discovery consists not in seeking new landscapes but in having new eyes.
MARCEL PROUST

~

So let the way wind up the hill or down,
O'er rough or smooth, the journey will be joy
Still seeking what I sought when but a boy,
New friendship, high adventure, and a crown,
My heart will keep the courage of the quest,
And hope the road's last turn will be the best.

HENRY VAN DYKE

~

~

~

~

~

The heavens declare the glory of God: the skies proclaim the work of His hands. Day after day they pour forth speech: night after night they display knowledge.

THE BOOK OF PSALMS

~

~

~